Help! I'm Sensitive

by Ronni Ann Hall

50 TOOLS FOR THE SENSITIVE TO HELP YOU SURVIVE AND THRIVE

From DESIGNING FAIRY

I think the next step is deflection, self defense. Rather than be so affected by negativity and take it in, I could fight it off and protect from it. I didn't learn that. I learned how to take care of other people's feelings instead.

Help! I'm Sensitive:

50 Tools for the Sensitive to Help You Survive and Thrive

By Ronni Ann Hall

Published by:

Designing Fairy

Book Division

Camp Verde, Arizona

http://thedesigningfairy.com

http://ronnispsychicroom.wordpress.com

http://www.ronnianndesigningfairy.com

Publishing Info

Copyright 2011 Ronni Ann Hall, a.k.a. Ronni Ann Roseman-Hall

All artwork and design: Ronni Ann Hall – Designing Fairy

Cover illustration: Butterfly Doctor by Ronni Ann Hall

Book One in the *Help for the Sensitive* series

Other books by Ronni Ann Hall:

For The Love of Dog (Chinup Chinook Books)

Word Swirls (Element Children's Books)

Are you a sensitive? quiz

This is the quiz I have on my website. I'm sure you will recognize yourself on this page.

1. Do you feel everyone else's emotions as if they were your own? Walk away from talking to a sad friend and are sad or tired and drained? Comfort an angry friend and are angry the rest of the day?

2. Do you know or can sense what an animal is thinking? Feel comfortable in Nature?

3. Are crowds exhausting to you? Do you lose your center when walking in a mall and start to feel overwhelmed?

4. Have you ever been told you are too sensitive? Need to "toughen up?" Do you care deeply about others and life?

5. Are you sensitive to the chemicals in food? Or in your laundry detergent? Or in the air?

6. Do you just "know" things and see things that others can't see?

7. Do you hear the news and it feels emotionally upsetting to you? After news of the recent earthquakes, tsunamis, did you feel overwhelmingly sad, or carry a vague sense of dis-ease? Felt off balance?

8. Do you need time alone at the end of the day or you feel crazy? Too many people overwhelm you and you start to feel nervous?

9. Do you sometimes feel like you need to shut everyone else's thoughts and feelings out?

10. Do you feel that your sensitivity is even increasing? Your psychic ability is increasing?

If you answered YES to most of these questions, welcome sensitive! You are an empath. It's wonderful being one if you learn how to balance your sensitivity and use your empathic ability as the gift it is.

Reviews for Help! I'm Sensitive:

"This is a lovely book, offering practical help in daily living for people who are sensitive and highly empathic. It is clearly written, well-organized and user-friendly, with tools that are easy to apply. Ronni's down-to-earth, humorous and non-threatening style of writing allows insight and learning to happen almost effortlessly. I would recommend this book to sensitive and empathic people who are trying to live with and manage their special gifts." — *Carolyn R. Moore, L.C.S.W.*

"When the student is ready the teacher comes. Well, this is so true with your book. I consider myself so blessed with my work and there was always this one place where I was most vulnerable, my sensing. I knew that before some of my sessions and after even days after, I would get physically ill--stomach aches, headaches and chest tightness are the most common. Sentience has always been my frenemy. I really truly appreciate the divine timing of finding your book. I have recommended it to so many others. It makes this real, it real, validates it for me and that it's no just a side effect of being a really rockin' psychic." – *Bridgette Doerr, seebridgette.com*

"I recommend Ronni Ann Hall's book for anyone learning to deal with their psychic sensitivities. Reading her book feels like listening to the advice and stories of a close friend…What I really love about Ronni's book is that she writes from personal experience. She gives so many examples of everyday situations that presented lessons for learning how to integrate and refine her empathic abilities." — *Jen LoveJoy, faeryhawkspeaks.blogspot.com*

"Ronni has a way of explaining how energy works from a very wise and clear place that is easy to understand and take-in. Just by the way she defines a "Sensitive" is so helpful and totally shifts any negative ideas one may have with being "Sensitive". — *Melissa Fernandez, spiritgoddess.com*

Table of Contents:

For Emma Lou and Sarah, my favorite teachers.

Special thanks to Caroline, Bill, Wendy, Pamela, and Jan Marie, who offered loving guidance and helped me learn these lessons.

A Letter to the Sensitive

You may have spent your whole life trying to shut your sensitivity down, like I did. Instead, the abilities surface through nervousness and anxiety, belly aches, or even depression.

You may have been told that you don't have these abilities and just want attention, but you have seen with amazing accuracy the validity of your perceptions.

You may have felt fear about your abilities, but you really do have control with them, once you have tools and understanding on how to use them.

You may have felt the backlash of your sensitivity living in an insensitive world–you're sensitive to foods, and the environment. Everything makes you rash out. Too many people overwhelm you. Those are the times you curse being you.

You may have felt an outsider in the world, and want to hide who you are just to fit in. But you forget, everyone has something a little different inside of them.

You may have felt very lonely as you deeply connect to everyone and everything on such a deep level, because they can't always return the favor.

You have these gifts for a reason. You were made this way for a bigger purpose. Embrace your gifts, because your path is one of self-acceptance. And once you reach that, and embrace all of you, you will truly save the world, one person at a time.

It is my hope that the following tools will help you find your balance again and repair what's been lost. Let's begin.

50 Tools

Definition of "Sensitive"

Important distinction: gentle soul does not mean delicate. You can be sensitive and intuitive and still be a source of strength and will. Throughout the course of this book, "sensitive" is in reference to how you are wired in body makeup and temperament.

Problem 1: **Your sensitivity**

Sensitive tool: **Identify you are an empath**

What exactly is a psychic empath? You know you are a psychic empath if:

- You walk into a room and you can feel if the air is heavy or light, if there was an argument in the room, or if someone is sad. Sometimes, this ability can be overwhelming.

- You walk down the mall and you feel unbalanced or unsteady from the barrage of other people's feelings and emotions.

- You know your dog or cat is feeling stressed or sad because you can feel it. Sometimes, you confuse the feeling as your own. You may even feel other people's ailments.

- You may have a sensitive stomach, or have reactive skin to the environment.

- Too much activity in your environment=crazy feelings inside you--nervousness, frustration, and major Attention Deficit Disorder.

- You can merge with a person, plant or animal, and see from its perspective.

- You tell yourself, or someone has told you, you are too sensitive and need to "toughen up."

Bottom line definition: psychic empaths experience the world from what they feel; and what they feel includes an enormous amount of psychic information ready to be tapped into. We see below the layers.

Problem 2: **Being an empath is unsafe**

Sensitive tool: **Having control of your abilities**

I was at a social gathering the other day eating coffee cake and chatting away, when a woman rushed over to me dragging a friend behind her. She introduced herself as a healer. The woman she was with then introduced herself as the woman's very enthusiastic student who was learning all she could on healing. When she asked what I did, I explained I was an empath who did readings and taught psychic classes.

You would think I just told the woman that I dumpster-dive for money.

"Oh no, you don't want to be *that*. In today's world with all the crazy energies, you can't be an empath."

This message was the equivalent of telling me I shouldn't be short or have green eyes.

Is that what the woman told herself? Don't be empathic, it's dangerous?

That answer is harmful. The more helpful one is to not close down your abilities, but to identify and embrace them while indulging in lots of self-care.

Throughout this book, I hope to include many tips on how to do this. But please don't think it is unsafe to be who you are as an empath. Shutting down your gifts helps no one.

Problem 3: **I get too involved with other people's lives.**

Sensitive tool: **Duck Energy**

For an empath, duck energy is essential–the key to sanity. Duck energy represents detaching from others' stuff and observing without carrying.

How do you know you are carrying? You are reacting and lost in another person's feelings, or taking personally their behavior.

Not too long ago in my life, I parented a child with many mental disorders, who was also knee-deep in adolescence. What a challenge, but a great way to learn *duck energy* hands-on.

Girls at that age are reactive at best, add bi-polar and personality disorder, and it's a nightmare. I remember at the time, telling my husband that it felt like she had premenstrual syndrome 24/7. My immediate response to anger is anger, so using duck energy had been a much better tool. Perhaps she was simply bringing up my trigger points. I'd watch her do absolutely nothing a few days straight and I'd want to step in and offer suggestions, help, anything. But I finally learned this act did nothing but aggravate her more. *Let it go*, I kept hearing. But as a parent, isn't it our jobs to make sure our girls grow up to be happy, well-adjusted adults? *Let it go.* Where's her passion? Her joy? Her excitement? *Let it go. Just swim along in the sea and don't get lost in others' floods. They are swimming along too, the best they can.*

Looking back at that experience, I realize it was important to create strong boundaries against her anger, which was abusive, and stating those boundaries what I would tolerate sent at me was the tool I needed and the first part of duck energy.

Using part two of duck energy--Compassionate Detachment-- I could try to understand where she was coming from and why she was how she was--by using my empathic gifts to hear or know—which would allow me to stay in compassion and in a higher perspective, and therefore, not take on those feelings or react as if it *was* personal.

~

Problem 4: **Losing yourself around others**

Sensitive tool: *Everything I Love* book

Yesterday I was in THE worse mood possible. I didn't know what was wrong with me! I was so angry and depressed. Being an empath, I concluded I probably picked up someone else's stuff again unwillingly. I was just plain negative. You know you are doing this when the bad mood comes out of nowhere. Your head might even ache. So, I sat down with my Spiritual Guides and Helpers and I heard what I was experiencing was "residue from others." I didn't know how I felt or what I wanted, and I was confused! So, I asked for guidance, and I was directed to make an "Everything I love" book. I was to cut out from magazines images that interested me, called to my soul, and represented what I truly loved right now.

Bringing the energy and focus back to myself, I felt me again and not the room around me.

I cut out images of beautiful paintings, costumes, books, colors, the Ghost Hunter series (everyone knows I love that), and patterns emerged. The path was clearer what *I* wanted. I cried and cried. *Ah, there's my spirit!*

As an empath and a sensitive, I find I may merge too much with what is around me and I lose myself. Creating my "Everything I love" book, re-centered my focus back to me, which for empaths, can be one of the biggest challenges.

Incidentally, another conclusion that I came to while making the book, was that I was forcing myself to do what I think I should do in my life, rather than what I wanted to do (we will cover this in the PONY SHOW entry). Henceforth, the old bad feelings were there in me, which attracted the bad feelings of those around me.

Problem 5: **Listening to your head for guidance,**

not your heart

Sensitive tool: **Your empathic gift**

I am learning the difference between wise will connected to my higher self, and lower will connected to my little brain, according to the great book *Spiritual Growth* by Sanaya Roman.

On my journeys, I stopped at a local healer's place and tried out a fabulous essential oil, Cardamom. With just a little rub, I felt grounded and calm. That's the great thing about being a sensitive, a little goes a long way! The healer, Suzanne, noticed I started coughing. She said that meant my feelings were not aligned with my head. I've been working on head-only decisions, and have only lately been learning how to follow my intuition or heart/feelings, according to Sanaya, which is my wise will. The wise will leads you through your feelings and what you WANT to do. As empaths and sensitives, we have a built-in guidance center: our feelings. They are powerful and accurate. Bypassing them and using only your head, is ignoring this important tool.

Today I feel like painting canvases and making flower essences. My brain is telling me to go fuss on the website and worry some more. Which do you think I will listen to?

~

Problem 6: **Dealing with non-empathic people**

Sensitive tool: **Acceptance**

I recall an experience with the counselor of my former daughter that revealed to me that not everyone is empathic. Because I see the world through my eyes, I often assume they are empathic also. Just because I live at a level of deep feeling and knowing, doesn't mean everyone else does. This can be frustrating. I thought this woman, who appeared to be a good counselor for the child, understood what I was describing and feeling, but then she said something that revealed she didn't get it at all! She thought she did, but she didn't. She was even very left field. I thought if she had really heard, put all the obvious pieces together, and SEEN, like I always do, she would have gotten it.

Being empathic can be difficult. We see many layers simultaneously at once. We can often feel what others are feeling and understand the big picture easily.

You KNOW your friend isn't upset about the phone bill, but her lack of communication with her family. You KNOW the real issues, the real problem. Our frustration can be when others can't return the favor; when they had no idea we felt that way. *We have to tell them.*

I often think that in previous lifetimes I must have been a no-nonsense, all-logic, non-feeling type, and this lifetime is my karma. Or, seeing more positively, this is my learning experience to create some soul balance by living as a feeler.

Next time someone cocks their head at you in confusion, remind yourself everyone is different. You have a gift they may be missing, and vice versa.

Problem 7: **Emotions coming up to the surface and overwhelming you**

Sensitive tool: **Flower essences for the sensitive**

The other day, I felt besieged by feelings and pictures in my head of an earlier time and crisis. The emotions were so strong, I would have thought I was back there in that time period.

As sensitives, we do a great deal of spiritual work on ourselves to heal and clear. The good news is when the emotions and feelings are so close to the surface, those leftover feelings are ready to leave. And when you are releasing that issue, those feelings are the strongest. I liken this to when you have a cut on your hand. It always looks crusty and yucky and even itches right before it finally heals. That's good news. The problem is when we get lost in what we are releasing, *all over again*. There is no need to replay. That's why there are the tools of flower essences to help make the release gentler and easier.

I am often asked what flower essences are really good for empaths and can help with this process. Here are my favorites:

1. **Calendula/Marigold**. I discovered this one with the help of the Nature Spirits. It balances out what's your stuff and what is others'. This one is good to take to protect yourself while you are dealing with your own stuff, so you don't add the weight of carrying others.
2. **Yarrow.** Any kind of Yarrow is great for the Sensitive. It's protection. It creates that nice bubble around you so you don't feel bombarded from the world. When you are releasing, you are vulnerable and need a protective cocoon to allow you to heal.
3. **Lavender.** This flower was made for the Sensitive! Its healing qualities buffer your nervous system. We take so much in even in the course of a day. All the layers that are happening

we see and feel. At the end of the day you need an un-ruffling.

4. **Any kind of Rose essence**. Roses carry a higher vibration, so that means they will uplift and carry you up with them. That's nice and needed so you don't get lost in the negativity of what you are experiencing.

5. **Salvia**. Salvia is great for emotional calming. High emotions go along with high sensitivity, so I like this one for any time I need calming down. Salvia will turn down the intensity of the emotions you are releasing, so they are doable.

How do you use a flower essence? Just put a few drops into your water for sipping or under the tongue, once a day. Flower essences are non-toxic and non-chemical, purely vibrational, so therefore, are perfect for sensitive systems.

~

Problem 8: **Empathic warnings**
Sensitive tool: **Listening to your body**

What if our bodies warn us ahead of time when an event or situation won't be good for us? And what if we've been ignoring this inner barometer all along?

Recently, I had to drive to such a situation late at night. I was pretty tired to begin with after a long day, and after being on a "mom" schedule for five years, I wasn't used to staying up late! (I know, I know, pretty sad). I've had to drive quite a bit at night lately, and unfortunately, don't have the night vision I wish I had, but it was still doable.

Driving over to the destination, the first thing that happened was a deep feeling of dread followed by a stomach ache. (Sensitive folks, take note! Our stomachs are like built-in radars). I couldn't throw off the feeling or the anxiety I was feeling. So preoccupied with my feelings, I missed my exit on the highway, something I've never done before! Halfway to Phoenix and driving the wrong way, I went into a panic. I almost experienced a full-fledged panic attack but remembered to deep breathe. I was dissociating, a little out of my body.

Somehow I managed to get back to my exit and to the direction of my original destination. Now, keep in mind, there's a fear/excited feeling vs. a dread/fear feeling. The second one is your warning that where you are heading won't be a good fit. Turns out, it was not! If I had only listened to my spot-on internal radar.

Oh, and to add, you should never feel in a situation, like the third man out, discounted, and ignored, ever. We often rationalize that we need to stay in these situations to learn something, or endure to be a good person, etc. But I am realizing that this is untrue. These feelings are pointing you to the exit door, or a reassessment of your situation to make sure your needs are included.

Problem 9: **Inner child reacting**

Sensitive tool: **Recognizing clues**

With what I realized the other day, I am amazed that anyone gets along with anyone else.

Often, we are reacting constantly to triggers from childhood, and are reliving patterns. Feel abandoned when a loved one doesn't call? That's just your inner child who felt abandoned when Mom and Dad traveled a lot. Angry at your spouse when she asks for compliments? There's Mom when you were a kid being over-controlling with her need for attention and reassurance from her children.

How do you know it is your inner child reacting? Your emotions and feelings may not be logical. The emotional level of your reactionary space is of a small child and reflects a small child's thinking. Children always feel that everything is their fault and that the world revolves around them. It's distorted beliefs that change with adulthood, but some get left behind.

Old environments will pull you into old roles where you feel like a kid again. You will feel like you haven't moved forward at all in your life, but this is only an illusion.

The tool here is to recognize that you are being triggered. Take a deep breath, and stand back when you are upset with someone's behavior. Is your adult reacting or your inner child? When you recognize the old wounds, you can move one giant step forward and change the dynamics in your relationships to ones that work. When you shift, others can too. Then give your child what she didn't get every chance you can. That's the cool part: you can re-parent yourself.

So, a good rule of thumb that you are dealing with your inner child is, *if it's heavy, it's old.*

Problem 10: **Nightmares after watching television**
Sensitive tool: **Watch what you watch**

After a long day participating in an art show, I came home exhausted, and instead of relaxing and unloading, I did the opposite of self-care. I watched an episode of *Paranormal State*. Ordinarily, I like that show and it's good entertainment, but, I was pretty open and excited from the effects of the art show that included leftover nerves and being exposed to a lot of people's energies. My best defense should have been to relax and clear out. But, no, being an excitement-seeking sensitive, I grabbed for more stimulation.

As I mentioned, I like that show. I love when Chip Coffey, the medium, comes in and gives his psychic hits. And, I love how the gang of college investigators comes in to help the family in need. What I'm not thrilled about is when Lorraine Warren comes in and labels every haunting a demon. I'd love to label every bad feeling or impulse I've ever had as a demon, then I could simply exorcise myself. How cool would that be? Most entities haunting in the shows I watched in were not demons--in my opinion--but people's well-developed fears that became thought-forms, or in the case I watched, someone's mental illness. Other hauntings are just people--dead people--behaving badly, who need serious boundaries.

I think years ago, people were burning witches for psychic ability, and casting out demons from folks who had mental illness. Haven't we evolved a little more than that? Past our own fears? I guess as a teacher, my biggest frustration is lack of educated people. How quick many are to go into ignorance than find wisdom.

Needless to say, watching that show and being an open empath, stirred up my own fears and gave me nightmares. Much of the fear originated from the folks I was watching on television!

There were lots of lessons learned there. A reminder, as an empath, I need to give myself special self-care. With gifts, comes responsibility to take care of those gifts. I need to be careful about what I take in and that includes what shows I watch. Watching someone else's fear means I will be picking up on fear. Isn't it a better choice to surround myself with wisdom instead?

~

Problem 11: **Holding in negativity**

Tool: **Clearing it out gently**

Have some negativity to get rid of? Taken on someone else's stuff? My Guides and Helpers have taught me to hold a rock person. Ask the rock or crystal to transmute the negative energy you've taken on and send the energy into the rock as you hold it. When you feel complete, ask the rock what it needs to clear. You may intuitively pick up that the rock needs to sit in a window, or needs to set in a glass of sea salt. It may be a crystal that self-generates and never needs clearing. *(Wouldn't that be nice for us?)*

Other ways to clear out what isn't yours? Check out the grounding exercises I mention in this book.

I also do a meditation where I ask that anything that isn't mine to please leave, and then I call back any of my own energy I have lost to fill in those empty spaces.

Baths are amazing for centering back to ourselves and clearing out what we don't need. Add a little Epsom salts and you will feel sparkling new.

For a quick way to clear, grab a smudge stick of sage and wave the lit stick all over your body. This works for animals also, yet some do like to run off when they see the smoke. My basset hound, Emma Lou, is notorious for that.

Problem 12: **Focusing on everyone else**

Sensitive tool: **Focus on you**

I'm listening to a great tape–**Time Management from the Inside Out**–as I drive to teach classes at a local college. Of course, the suggestions on the tape are for the ideal situation. I find, lately, I rush around like a nut most days, bending to everyone else's needs, ending the day exhausted, and my own fun ends up on the back burner. I realized *my* time management was more about being centered for me in my own world–not pulled by the many threads around me. I learned this in Nia class the other day.

In Nia, a free-form type of dance class, we bend and flow and scurry around the room. When I switched focus to watch what the other dancers were doing, I actually lost my balance and fell! Back in my own head and body, and my own experience, I felt centered and strong. How fabulous a dance class would be so profound in teaching me. The way I approached my process in the class would apply to everything else I do. This week with the help of my ever-present and very patient spiritual helpers, I am focusing on centering back to me and focusing on *my* needs and goals.

~

Problem 13: **Sensitive skin**

Sensitive tool: **Soap for the Sensitive**

One of my frustrations from being a sensitive being, is having very sensitive, reactive skin. This means I have to be extra careful with what touches my skin, whether laundry detergent or my soap.

A few recommendations:

- *Cetaphil Soap*. Found in most drug stores, this soap is super gentle on the skin. I found that the one for Normal/Oily is best for removing makeup and dirt. The more gentler version takes many rubbings to remove makeup.

- Buy your laundry detergent marked as FREE. Not all brands are equal, so test each. If you are reactive to the detergent, you may notice your skin protesting in little red bumps or dots.

- Watch what you eat. When I eat too much sugar or white flour, I breakout. If I eat something that doesn't agree with me it will be both my stomach and my skin that scream out. Know your body and what it likes.

- For makeup, I like *Clinique* brand which I have found very gentle and less irritating on my skin. This brand was recommended to me by my mom years ago who also had sensitive skin.

Problem 14: **Headaches from sensitivity**

Sensitive tool: **Headache solutions**

I had the worst headache. I was only able to get rid of it by taking a nap and a dose of Tylenol, but I had a doozy of a time figuring out what caused it, until I had some time to do some healing on my head. Here are reasons why, if you are psychic or sensitive, you may have a headache:

- •1. **You're tired**. This was the simplest reason for me. I needed to rest.
- •2. **Hormones shifting**. That's for you, ladies, out there.
- •3. **My head will ache in my psychic spot if there's negativity around me in some form.**
- •4. **Sometimes your head aches when there's a spirit around of a lower or different vibration.** I've been to "haunted" places, and boy, it felt like my head would come off in some.
- •5. **Stuck emotions–your own.** I was upset yesterday and tried to hold it all in. Boy, can you get that doozy of a headache holding back the stream.
- •6. **Stuck emotions–others.** If you are empathic, you can take on others' stuck emotions–the ones they aren't expressing–and carry it. Ouch. Important to differentiate if it is yours or not. Ask that whatever isn't yours to leave, and if you feel better, you have evidence.
- •7. **For you hypochondriacs–brain tumor**. Just don't go there. If it's a really bad headache, we're talking huge, then go there.
- •8. **Too much energy in the head**–this happens to me often. Best way to take care of this? Ground it out somehow. Go do yoga, hold your feet, walk, take a flower essence, and get out of your head. Doing more head work, or worrying more, makes it worse.

- 9. **And last but not least, what did you eat or didn't eat?** I had sugar while my blood sugar was low. Whoops. Ouch. But it tasted really good.

~

Problem 15: **Cleaning up someone else's stuff**

Sensitive tool: **Owner Carry affirmation**

If you are practicing Duck Energy and compassionate detachment, and you still need another reminder, here's a good one.

In my caring, I want to make it better for my loved ones. I hate to see them suffer, and with my impatience, I try to jump right in and carry their load by taking care of what they need to take care of.

I wasn't backing off and was knee deep in others' lessons. I needed a bigger reminder.

Enter my elderly beagle girl, Sarah.

Unfortunately, Sarah has been forgetting all about her house-training. Part of the problem is she is blind and can't always find the door. The other part is being a beagle, which means being stubborn and doing what she wants to do.

I usually go to the Unity Center on Sundays and Sarah prefers me to be home in my office nearby her. It appears that when I am not home she waits by the door, relieves herself and then begins to pace back and forth. I'm sure you have the picture in your mind now of the giant mess that awaits me when I get home. One such time, as I was on my knees cleaning up the floor and cursing, I realized the obvious metaphor. I've been cleaning up other people's messes, and that had to stop.

Driving down the highway, I saw a huge realtor sign in front of a vacant lot that says "Owner Carry." When you are in a situation where someone you love is having a problem, remind yourself, *Owner Carry.* It's not yours, it's theirs, and you don't want to interfere with their lessons. Besides, when we rush in to help others, we give the message that the other person is not capable, and no one wants to be seen that way.

Problem 16: **Nonacceptance for being sensitive**

Sensitive tool: **Stand in your truth**

I've been very spoiled the last ten years. We've lived close to Sedona, the capital of weird and crazy psychic activity. Most of my friends are all intuitive in some way and see things from a higher perspective. It is not uncommon to speak about animal communication, or about our Guides and Angels in our normal conversation, because this is our reality. When my family moved away to an area that is beautiful and filled with more activity, we unknowingly moved into a small town that is very religious and church-going. My own family was very spiritual but not religious.

We took our one dog, Foxy, to a new veterinarian. A huge coincidence was the new vet just happens to be a vet I met long ago when she was just starting out, and I was just beginning my animal communication practice. I drew and designed her logo for her business, and in return, she did a house call for our dog babies. She believed in animal communication, alternative healing and flower essences, and even lived in a spiritual retreat center for some time.

We had a pleasant visit but then found out Foxy had kidney disease. Foxy herself had communicated to me that she felt her dog food was too rich and salty and was causing a strain on her kidneys. In the vet's office, I knew then, that she needed to recheck Foxy's kidneys, which was a correct message. The vet honored my intuitive ability.

At the end of the check-up, I felt great that I had finally found an aware vet. I left some business cards at the counter after paying the bill. Much to my surprise and amazement, I later received a phone call from the office manager saying I needed to remove my business cards because the owners are Christian and don't believe in that "stuff." Not missing a beat, I just suggested they give the cards to the vet we worked with who WAS into that kind of "stuff."

I am still amazed. Perhaps, I've been too sheltered being surrounded by like-mindeds for so long. I don't see how being a Christian excludes you from believing in healing with Nature and working with your intuition. Many of my students have a Christian background and believe fully in the power of intuition just from their experiences alone. Perhaps, I was sent there that day for reassurance for the vet we know. I am not sure if we should look for a new vet for our girls or not. I do know that I felt excluded and unaccepted for who I am. After all, God made me psychic, and that is not what Christianity is supposed to be about. Christ, I recall, was all about unconditional love and acceptance for everyone. And wasn't Christ himself able to talk to animals, heal with his hands, channel God and his messages?

When you encounter this kind of prejudice, speak and stand in your truth, and then kindly walk away. There are others in every field that do match you and will accept you for who you are. That's where you will feel not different at all.

~

Problem 17: **Psychic energy build-up**

Sensitive tool: **Let your abilities flow**

I am finding that now that I am doing much more readings, and swimming again, I am having much less headaches. Many times, I will have such a build-up in psychic energy that I will actually see sparks and energy in the air. I am wondering then, if by using my abilities I am working with the energies to flow through, so I am not experiencing such a backlash.

For so long I felt I'd try to be "normal" and mainstream myself, avoiding who I am. I can't. I am a very intuitive person. I need to use it and not fight it. Come out of the closet, so to speak, and say, this is what I do! No matter how freaky being psychic may be to some. The information I receive really helps people and their animals.

I used to watch the show *Ghost Whisperer*. On the show, the main character embraced her gift fully to help others, as painful & as frustrating as that can be sometimes. Her mother, on the other hand, denounced that ability, and had terrible headaches. Now I think it was from the build-up of energy that made her head hurt. Energy has to go somewhere.

But, I have also noticed, that when someone is particularly negative towards me or even if there is a spirit in the room bugging me, my head will ache in my psychic spot. Those headaches are warnings and are valuable. Once again I am reminded, that I need to really listen to my body, which has a psychic wisdom all its own.

Problem 18: **Merging with your environment**

Sensitive tool: **Nature as a remedy**

I haven't been in Nature for a great while. I went to the park today and I felt like an empty bottle filling up!

Why is Nature so good for empaths and sensitives? Because we tend to blend and merge with our environments to gather information. What better place to merge with then a park in Nature? Nature replenishes, gives back to us, and it is self-renewing. It gives us energy we can fill back up with, and in return, we give back our newly replenished positive energy and light to the world.

Problem 19: **I can't hear guidance!**

Sensitive tool: **Naps**

Fear blocks your answers. In my case, fear blocked my trust in what good guidance I was receiving. I was in a recent crisis with my dog's health. I was hearing several voices. Voices from my Guides and Helpers were mixed in with old voices learned from childhood, and outside voices giving me crappy and untruthful advice. With fear, old records are spinning around and around in your head. It's hard to see what is right and what is wrong for you. I found that the secret to get past all the gunk and the junk is to:

Rest!

I couldn't discern my truth when I had under-slept for two weeks. I was then ripe for fear to overtake me. With less sleep, there was less clarity and my emotions were running amok. Many times, we are out of touch with how *we* feel after spending a day focused on everyone else's feelings. After a good nap or excellent night's sleep, we re-center and come back to ourselves and our heads are clear!

Go take a nap. It's good for you.

~

Problem 20: **Uncomfortable energy**

Sensitive tool: **Recognizing energy**

One of the most important skills you have as an empath is to be able to recognize energy and how it makes you feel. Recognizing energy allows you to decide what you will let in and keep out.

I am one of those folks who believe it when I see it, or in this case, feel it. I suppose that is why I have in the last few years seen quite a few miraculous things. The other night, I was wide open, traveling in meditation, and had the amazing discovery that we are all energy or vibrations like stations on a radio. Okay, now we all know this. We've read it, heard it. But it was the first time I *really* felt it–it was exaggerated.

Sarah, my beagle mix, jumped on the bed with her morning nervous energy. I felt her static, hyper energy, that to me, felt physically very uncomfortable. I winced. I felt it on my own body as nervousness; that jumpy feeling. Then Emma Lou, my basset hound, jumped on the bed and her energy or radio station felt like it was set to "calm" or "elevator music." Her energy was flowing and felt gentle and soft and very comfortable to me. I realized on the microscopic feeling level, that is why some folks resonate with us and some don't, although we are not consciously aware of it.

I've been enrolled in a DVD-making class at the college. The other night, we watched my classmates' current video creations. Our assignment was to edit film clips to accompany a piece of music of our choosing. Several of the movies were hard for me to watch. There was flashing, hard images and loud, jarring music. My eyes and ears felt assaulted.

Some folks' energy are like this to me, only because my energy is different, although I do have days when my energy is like Sarah's morning energy, and I suppose to Emma Lou, I am very jarring. Those days Emma doesn't dig the music I am playing.

Problem 21: **Good vs. bad energy**

Sensitive tool: **Recognizing kinds of energy**

Today I felt the difference between receiving good energy and bad energy. Good energy-wise: I received my daily message from Tut.com. I felt uplifted, powerful, and excited to move on = good energy. I also received a very lovely blog review recognizing my blog as helpful = another warm, good, fuzzy feeling. On the other hand, for the first time, I received--I should feel flattered my blog is gaining such popularity--a very off, critical and not very helpful blog comment. I questioned myself, felt slimy, and wanted to go into bad OCD-like driven behaviors = bad energy. Sometimes, criticism is a good thing if it makes your work or services better. Good criticism might feel a little ouch-y at the time, but you know it is true. Bad criticism just doesn't feel good. It isn't helpful.

I would have stayed at the lesson right there, but BAM. I took the empath's way and was reminded to go deeper. This same criticism I received was what I tell myself often–that if something isn't working how I'd like it, I must not be doing it "right." So, I need to excessively obsess over things and work harder until whatever I am working on is "right." It was as if this person came along to show me this! This was old stuff and old patterns that didn't make sense anymore.

The truth for me, I have found, is those who are right for your work, your services, or business, "get" what you do right away. They already think it is right in every way, because it is meant for *them*. Haven't you noticed this? The others will weed themselves out by asking for what you can't give, wanting you to compromise more, and will want what you offer to be much different than what it is. I suppose this applies to relationships and life also. What do you think? We can say YES to the good energy.

Problem 22: **Bombardment of energies**

Sensitive tool: **Shut it off.**

Once you are recognizing energy, you may find times that you feel bombarded with too much.

I am writing about this helpful tool as I sit in a crowded, noisy library. It's hard to block out the many voices. It's like that with energy. When we are tired or worn down, all the energies around us swoops into us like we are giant sponges. How do you balance then?

Have you ever, as a kid, been so passionate and mesmerized by something that the world disappeared? That your mother called you for lunch many times and you didn't even hear her? You already knew the secret.

Find something that will give you that wonderful tunnel-vision focus. I know if I start to draw, or read a book on psychic ability, I'm gone; lost in my passion. I am blocking out the rest of the world. (A little secret -- that happens also when I read *Entertainment Weekly* and read all the gossip.) This tip also works great in scary, crowded airports.

Problem 23: **Depression**

Sensitive tool: **Take Notice**

Sensitive folk are prone to depression. Many times the emotion that registers as "depression" is a conglomerate of all the negative cast-offs from everyone else! As empaths and sensitives, we can reach out too much, be too compassionate and open, and being the sponges that we are, the next thing you know, you are carrying around other folks' stuff. (This can even happen from watching the news or soap operas!) Do this enough and depression is what you feel.

How do you know you took on others' stuff? You will know you are doing this when the mood hits you like a brick. One minute you are feeling fine and the next you wonder why you don't jump off the roof. It will be that sudden. And the depression will feel like a cloud or a veil covering you that you can't shake off.

Once you notice this, you can get out from under the cloud of others' doom. The tool here is to notice that drastic change in mood.

Start to see where and how you are exposed to negativity and try to reduce your exposure to it. If this has been happening for a long time, and the depression is severe, reach out for help. Find a good therapist to sort out what isn't yours and what is. Find a good healer to clear out the gunk.

And for self-clearing it out, go to Tool #21.

Problem 24: **My needs aren't met but I take care of everyone else's needs**

Sensitive tool: **Don't compromise affirmation**

Not too long ago in my life, I had what the tarot deck would call a Tower Experience, where life turns upside down for a while to stir things up. We tend to have life reviews when this happens, then we see a time-line of false beliefs that led us to that experience what we did not want to experience. I think that is the true gift in major life shake-ups.

What did I learn? For one thing, we must not compromise so much of ourselves. Each little compromise tells us we don't matter and are unimportant. And slowly, we learn to expect less and less. Next thing that happens is our reality shows us we matter little in our lives. We are disrespected. It's a snowball effect.

I look back and I see how all this was born when I was quite little. A belief was planted. And yes, Empaths, we do tend to take on others' beliefs and feelings as our own at a very early age.

I have seen times in my life where I gave 110% in my biz, my family, in parenting, relationships, and then was genuinely surprised when I was empty-handed. I foolishly thought that when I needed it, like financial help for my dying dog, or needing money for simple things like gas or electric, it would be there, because look how much I gave! I think all these experiences only created resentment. Why was this happening? One reason was I gave it out for free. I was such a good, old girl.

Helpers, when has anyone asked a dentist or electrician for free help? I saw this recently when a woman wanted a basically dirt-cheap reading for me to travel an hour and a half and talk to most of her dog kennel. Then she had the nerve to balk at my average price. It wasn't the matter of her not being able to pay. She had just paid a vet to come to the house big bucks! So, the message again was, you are unimportant, not worthy. That was part of my wake-up call. Somewhere in the equation I learned my needs didn't matter. And when I didn't acknowledge my needs, and compromised by putting the needs of others first, I attracted others who reflected that belief.

Little by little, we put up with small compromises in our day that do not honor us and whittle us away. Maybe this is a learned woman thing. I don't know. But it's too late. I see it now. I have this beautiful opportunity to rewrite this belief.

New belief: My needs matter just as much as whom I serve.

~

Problem 25: **Holes are our weak spots**

Sensitive tool: **Recognizing holes**

Holes inside us make us vulnerable to taking things personally.

We all came into this world with a mission, and at the same time, a hole to work on filling, that's what I learned.

A hole is formed in childhood, or even carried over from a past life. It's our Achilles heel; (or Achilles *heal*) our weakest spot. The key to filling holes is not to ignore them, or throw junk food or alcohol in them to fill them, but to work *with* them. Because what lies within our holes, lives treasure.

Long ago, I learned falsely that what I really wanted, I couldn't have, and therefore, that my needs were forgotten. It was the creation of my hole.

Now, I find myself in the current position of lacking trust that I will get what I most need and that I'll be taken care of financially, another view from my hole.

If I choose to work with my hole, I need to see that I grow impatient and angry when I think that I won't be taken care of. I get lost in fear. My hole becomes the size of Grand Canyon.

What do I do? I give myself small tasks to do and then I reward myself. If I feel like nothing I do is enough, I appreciate myself and make a big deal of every small accomplishment I do. I give myself a bubble bath for writing those tough articles; I buy fancy frames for my paintings; I put my drawings on the refrigerator with happy face magnets. I take advantage and use what I have. I may take a bubble bath or bake from what is in the pantry. I spoil myself and feel the abundance right here.

Understanding the origins of my distrust, I don't trust blindly, instead I give myself some compassion. I ask the universe to work with me in small steps showing me the world is trustworthy and wants what I want. I keep track of experiences when I was given what I needed when I needed it. I take baby steps to learn trust again.

With the awareness of what we didn't get and what we now need, we are in a better position to work with our holes and begin to put our energy into our missions and what we are here for.

Here's an interesting thought: our greatest gift to ourselves and others resides *in* our holes. What we have experienced and healed is what we can teach others, and therein lies our mission.

~

Problem 26: **I am being drained**

Sensitive Tool: **What is a psychic vampire and how they are made**

The danger of having holes is that we are walking around with wide-open spaces inside of us, inviting others to plug into our holes and take advantage. With my need for recognition, I attracted someone who tried to mold me into what they wanted me to be in exchange for some much needed appreciation. It was difficult to untangle from this person and the situation, but I did. I realized later that situation would never have filled in my hole, only made it worse by not providing the real food I needed.

That was my first experience with a psychic vampire.

What are psychic vampires and how are they made? Some folks have had awful childhoods. They didn't receive what they needed at an early age. A child is smart. It is adaptive, and in survival, figures out how to get what it needs. Mom doesn't pay attention to me when I cry, but when I push her cereal bowl off the table, she runs over to me. It may be negative attention but it's still attention. An adaptive fill-in-the-hole strategy has occurred. The child fills in the holes with new beliefs and behaviors on how to get what she/he needs.

Later in life, this same child grows and learns from that earlier experience that feeling love and getting attention is only through upsetting others greatly. Henceforth, a psychic vampire is born draining others around her to get what she needs. She leaves chaos and upset wherever she goes, but she doesn't understand that there is another way to do this. There is so much missing in her that she can't survive without living off someone else's energy. If she is open to it, as an adult she may learn this doesn't work and find a new, healthier way to get her needs met. If she doesn't, she continues to wreak havoc on the surrounding countryside draining left and right inspiring many to wear garlic around their necks.

As an empath, you are her favorite food. You are open and trusting and feel what everyone feels. You may even carry her pain for her in an attempt to help because you see those holes.

Don't. You aren't helping, you're hurting and draining *you* which is taking away any power you have, and she isn't getting any better by you enabling her. This is not your job to fix.

Most recently I learned with help, don't bargain with the vampire. If she could bargain or reason, or even hear you, she wouldn't be a vampire. Identify a vampire, send her some love, and then walk away.

And one more thing to add, there are vampires in every field. Just because someone is a therapist or a healer, she can still be one. Trust your feelings on this one.

~

Problem 27: **Psychic vampires getting in your holes**

Sensitive tool: **Tackle the fear with Mouse Theory**

We've covered how psychic vampires are made. This summer I had it hit home how they work.

I had mice in my house. I live in a relatively rural area with a lovely nature-filled backyard that I love. The first mouse that visited was cute and not much of a bother. I was kind to it. He brought others. And more others. And lots more others. These little guys liked my birds' cage and would cuddle in their fuzzy, pink blanket that I used to cover their cage at night. It was no longer cute when in the mornings I'd take the blanket off and have to relocate the little guys out into the field. Gratefully, I have a very nice landlord couple that responded quickly to my dilemma. Their question was, "How are they getting in?"

We covered up the holes everywhere and later found out that the mice were initially attracted to the neighbor's chicken feed next door. They had recently moved and taken the chickens with them. The mice, loving the bird seed, were looking for a new food source and somehow discovered my little old bird cage through a hole in the floor. My poor parakeets were not happy.

This experience came in perfect time for me to write this book. I was introduced to Mouse Theory. Mouse Theory asks you how are the psychic vampires getting in? Remember how we talked about holes? Those folks are pushing all your buttons and bringing up fears.

The answer or solution is to tackle those fears so they have no ammunition against you to use to get in.

I was being psychically attacked at the time I was experiencing Mouse Theory. I had awful fears come into my head coming from another person. Like the mice, she was attracted to my energy for safety, and what she thought I could give her.

I had to tackle the fears. Were they real? What did they say about me? After many talks with my Guides and Angels and seeing all of what information they gave me as validated, I realized that the fears coming at me, were far from reality. I educated myself. As I rose above and saw the big picture of my life, the fears dissipated even more. This particular person, when she was in a relationship with me, would try to get my attention by upsetting me. How fascinating that she could still do this through the astral world psychically through our prior connection.

After tackling the fears, I did a meditation to cut those psychic cords she may have had in me. I looked down at my body and saw clairvoyantly where they were and then gently visualized the cords dissolving with silver light. In the spaces where the cords were pulled, I imagined white, protective light going back in because there were now open spaces. I then created a strong instruction to all my doorkeepers that this person was not welcome in my space and imagined big walls around me. I have not felt her since.

Plug up your holes and set some boundaries. One mouse is cute, plural are not. Much like the fears, one fear is a nuisance, but many can cause some serious damage. You should see my books on the shelf where the mice liked to hang out.

~

Problem 28: **Dealing with another person's mental illness**

Sensitive tool: **Recognizing psychic ability vs. mental illness in others**

Let's talk about another form of vampires...do you know the difference?

After parenting an adopted child for five years who had tons of both, I slowly learned what the difference was, and that mental illness did not look how I thought it would. I always thought illness would be very obvious--like what we see on television--the bag lady in the street pushing the cart, or the man being carried away in the white strait jacket. What we thought was charming quirkiness in Jenny* early on, was clear-cut signs of mental illness that everyone poo-poo'ed away (many for their own agendas). Once adolescence kicked in, we had full-blown "lots of things." And honey, that was no ADHD, which we were originally told.

There is hearing voices of Guides/Angels or spirits in the room, and then there is hearing voices of your other personalities, split- off parts, or out-and-out schizophrenia. A good indicator these are not Guides? The voices aren't helpful. These voices may even try to get a rise out of you to get you upset (this could be earthbound spirits. They like to do that). Guides/Angels are always loving and when you hear their guidance you feel a sense of rightness and an inner-knowing. They are much like a good psychic reading. You don't have a reading and hear "you are going to die!" The psychic will tell you that you need to be more careful when you drive. Guides/Angels will never say nasty things about other people or tell you to hurt them in any way. Their drive is to help you have understanding and compassion for others. (The exception is a departed relative visiting who might give advice. Usually, you can identify the voice and how they always acted when they were alive.)

Jenny* would talk to voices in her room often and claim they were Guides, but I saw and felt nothing, except, I would have the beginning of a migraine when I entered. (Keep in mind though, earthbounds are attracted to high energy emotional states. I think she did have a few entities attached to her on top of everything else. Henceforth, my headaches).

Folks with personality disorders are really hard to peg as mentally ill. That's the tough part. Borderlines (called RAD when they are young) will take your life onto a roller coaster, one moment idolizing you when you do what they want, and the next, despising you for not complying. They are also masters of triangulation pitting one person against another just for the drama of it, because chaos feels safe. On the surface, they are as charming as can be, and always who they think you want them to be. But without treatment or help, their lives are a continuous, bad amusement park ride, and you don't need to join them, or risk developing your own mental illness.

When I first came to the Sedona area, one of the first things I did was readings at a healing fair. My first customer was a schizophrenic who wanted to know about the implants attached to his head controlled by the government. I did give him the benefit of the doubt after watching years of X-files, but his wife later confirmed he had mental illness. There was also a girl who claimed she was a reincarnated Jesus (lots of those). What scares me is many folks like this need medication or psychological help and not a psychic reading. Sedona is notorious for attracting all kinds of people who want healing. I got an instant education what to look out for.

If you do hear voices that are not helpful, find your moods seriously erratic, go get some help. Get educated. Our bodies and minds are so complicated. Sometimes it's just a hormone imbalance! We all have the ability to go a little off kilter in the most stressful times. (I've got a bit of OCD inherited from my grandmother. Thanks Nanny!)

And if you have more of a psychic intruder bothering you? Being a sensitive/psychic you could open some doors you don't need to open to outside unhelpful energies attracted to your bright light. Learn clearing exercises and find someone who specializes in escorting them out. I always call in Archangel Michael for the small jobs.

Problem 29: **Addictions**

Sensitive tool: **Retool**

We talked about filling holes made from childhood. As children, we did the best we could. Without the proper guidance on how to take care of our needs, we maladapted, and an addiction was born. The addiction served the need's purpose. Now as an adult, we grab for the addiction whenever our buttons are pushed, and those familiar yet very uncomfortable feelings from childhood rears its head. We don't want to feel.

I wish addictions were cured overnight but it can take some time. The key is to retool, much like we are doing with this e-book. Educate yourself as much as possible about your addiction. Find support with some kind of group or 12 step program. Take the maladaptive behavior and replace with a healthier one that fills your holes and your needs.

It's worth the work and part of the process of re-parenting your inner, little empath.

~

Problem 30: **I can't connect to my animals**

Sensitive tool: **Feeling their energy**

Now that you are recognizing energy, you can use this important skill to locate and feel your animals.

Every day, I take Speedy the tortoise out of his cage and plop him down on the floor. He usually makes a few rounds around the house before venturing through the pet door (yes, he uses the dog door), down the pet ramp meant for Sarah (who still doesn't use it), and into the yard. Most of the problem happens when I am not watching him and have to determine if he is in the house or outside the house. That isn't always easy–he hides behind doors, between the washer and dryer, and under beds, just for fun, or to mess with me.

Today, as I was working on my website, Speedy made it out the door. Halfway through working, I heard "The Turtle!" *(probably from Emma Lou)*. Searching the house, I couldn't find him anywhere. I grabbed Emma Lou and we couldn't find him outside either. (Emma was so cute. When I asked her to find the turtle she barked a few times, calling him.) This was unusual because he is usually visible walking somewhere in the yard.

I said a little prayer to my Angels and in exasperation, I sat down on a tie next to the swing on the ground. Right next to me, *literally* next to me, half hidden under a pile of leaves, I saw a hint of a turtle shell! He was right next to me! If I hadn't set down for a moment, I wouldn't have found him.

Was it a weird coincidence? Well, no. I felt his energy. I registered that energy on an empathic level and then I was pulled to that energy. It's using advanced empathy to connect to love ones and it is very helpful for finding lost animals. If I had used only my head, I'd still be looking, I am sure.

Problem 31: **I feel ungrounded from too much change.**

Sensitive tool: **Anchors & touchstones**

In this crazy world today with so much change, it is easy to feel *very* ungrounded. We may reach for equally crazy things to correct the balance or to feel more stable, such as overeating, or over-shopping, or even codependent behavior (us healer/empath types love to grab for this). It's as if we are thrashing about in the sea around us with no life preserver, so we are trying to find one.

The solution is to create **ANCHORS**.

What helps you feel more grounded?

Here are some ideas:

1. **Create structure.** As a Capricorn, my natural gift is to build and create structure. Structure can be as simple as having a routine you do every day, such as waking up in the morning having coffee and sitting in your yard. Or, having a writing schedule. It could be riding a bike every day after dinner. My favorite has been my evening routine sitting in my reading room with my dogs watching Project Runway. (Emma Lou loves the dress designs.)

2. **Friends**. An anchor can be a friend you regularly check in with. The more friends the better. They are probably feeling as ungrounded as you are nowadays, so you may be an anchor for them.

3. **Check in with yourself**. I suppose this is the same as centering, but I think anything that allows you to check back in with what *you* want, feel and need, is good. I journal. Visual journaling has been very helpful to me, and even just making lists of what I want to do or would like to do brings me back to me.

4. **Baby steps**. Sensitive folk need change gradually in their lives. This isn't always possible, but in regards to what you do have control over, make small steps. Don't rush it.

5. **And finally, pets.** Go play with your animals! Animals take you into the present moment and help you get grounded. They are also easily counted on and constants in our lives among lots of change.

~

Problem 32: **Empathic overload**
Sensitive tool: **Turtle shell**

I love teaching workshops. When I was teaching at the college, I met a lovely student who owned an animal rescue, and she wanted me to conduct an animal communication workshop at her place. I jumped at the chance to have the opportunity to be with animals and teach.

Karan's place was amazing: tons of fenced-in areas with horses, goats, and mules. She has many dogs that roam her property ready for pets and conversations. My heart opened wide from being with such great company.

She introduced me to a horse that was having some emotional issues with the other horses he was sharing the field with. As per my usual routine, I opened up and connected with the horse to feel his feelings and communicate. The session went very well. Then I did a big animal communication/empath no-no. I stayed open. It was like having my front door open and anyone could come in.

When I was ready to teach and address the group, I felt pure panic. Not from teaching, but because I now had about thirty animals who saw me talking to the horse and wanted to be next. Being wide open and merging with the environment, I now felt all those animals coming at me, and I felt what they felt, and could hear their voices.

I excused myself and found a quiet, alone space and did a quick meditation to pull all my energy back in as if I were a turtle going back into my shell. I asked that anything that wasn't mine, to leave, and basically created an energetic boundary around me. I then imagined a turtle shell of protection surrounding me that would create a filter so I could decide what came into my space. I set a strong intention that only who I wanted to talk to at that time would be my focus. I would reaffirm this by creating a bubble in my mind of privacy with whatever animal I was talking to.

The rest of the day went much better and it was a great reminder for me to go into that kind of situation with bubbles and a shell in place rather than having to do this exercise in an emergency.

When I was a young adult, I experienced panic attacks. This was a large factor—being too open and taking in too much-- in having those. It's great to be open, but not that open.

I used to also have this problem when walking in malls. Besides having so many energies to pick up from, most mall buildings are very contained with no windows to have energy to escape. Everything is packed in like a tuna fish container. As a Sensitive, you are registering all of those energies at once. The best protection is to visit outside malls, or put on your turtle shell before you enter to create that necessary filter.

~

Problem 33: **Bubbles are not enough**

Sensitive tool: **Archangel Michael as doorkeeper**

Last summer I took a class in Mediumship with Tina Daly and Charles Virtue. In a private conversation with Tina, I asked her about psychic boundaries and I explained how I was feeling bombarded with too many voices from other-worldly visits at night. She taught me one psychic tool that has made a huge difference in my life. Have a doorkeeper, she told me. And for extra protection, make Archangel Michael your doorkeeper. Archangel Michael's job is as the warrior of protection. He was all too happy to step in and protect me. I gave him strong instructions to let out lower energies and let me know who was knocking at my door. Since he was appointed to his new job, I noticed a silence I hadn't had in years! Originally, I would hear or see a face of who was connecting to me. Now it's evolved to a knowing who it is. Have the best on your side working for you.

Problem 34: **Carrying old pictures of ourselves in our auras**

Sensitive tool: **Change the pictures**

Sarah, my beagle mix who I've mentioned, used to have very poor self-esteem. She was a stray that found her way to us and still felt left-over abandonment issues.

Whenever Sarah would come to snuggle me I would have the oddest thoughts come in my head.

> *"Oh, Sarah isn't as special as Emma Lou (our basset hound)."*
>
> *"Sarah isn't very pretty."*
>
> *"Sarah isn't special at all."*

These thoughts were foreign to me as I felt she was just as special as Emma in her own way, and was a pretty dog. So, what was going on here?

We carry old pictures and thoughts around us in our auras. This old perception of herself that she had from her prior home was being dragged around with her to our home. We didn't feel that way, but her aura still had the picture in it that I could pick up subconsciously and react to.

Do you have old pictures you carry from childhood? You may be attracting people or situations that mirror those back to you, so you will change it. Feels awful, right? That's because those pictures aren't supposed to be there.

Sarah began to feel better once her confidence grew and we told her enough how special she really was. She changed with the new picture we had for her, and she was willing and able to release the old one.

Problem 35: **Using anger to separate you**

Sensitive tool: **Use your voice**

A sure sign that someone is trying to steal your energy or "get in" to your space is that you feel anger. Anger can be a beautiful and helpful tool to keep out what you don't want, if used wisely and recognized. That anger is indicating that someone has plowed through your boundaries. It's the warning system that is healthy to have. Don't dismiss it. Too many times I just explained it away and told myself I was overreacting. Sure enough, I'd later find out that my anger was justified.

Then there are times when you might use anger to get some space. As an empath, I blend too easily into another's space. When this became too cramped, I would get snippy and upset and push away by getting angry. The mad mood would bubble to the surface as a form of protection.

The key is to use my voice and express my boundaries and needs when I feel this happen. It's tough to do when you are used to always pleasing others and don't want to hurt feelings, but you are helping others by letting them know what you need and therefore, how you can be your best and happiest. If someone loves or cares about you, they want to know this! Saying you need alone space is a right you have.

And, if you are ever in a situation that feels too crowded, like a party, and you find yourself getting bitchy and short, head to the bathroom. You are guaranteed to be alone and have the space you need, and no one will question why you were in there.

~

Problem 36: **Molding and the pony show**

Sensitive tool: **Just be you**

Perhaps you can resonate with my "hole." Many empaths are the good kids growing up that are no problem, or the ones that take care of the other kids. We can be the pleasers and will often mold into what we think others want us to be. I call this the "pony show."

As adults, you may find that you are miserable in your accounting job because you are a musician with a head for notes, not numbers. You live in snowy New York because that is where your family lives and has always lived, but you yearn for the red rocks.

By molding to what others want, especially when you can intuit what that image looks like, you make others happy, but you abandon yourself. Sooner or later, you will feel this by your depression, your illness, or your lack of will to live.

Leave behind the pony show. You are not here to please anyone but yourself.

(As an added tool, check out the Myers Briggs classifications. Sometimes your "type" doesn't mesh with the job or situation you are in.)

Problem 37: **Being in the trenches**

Sensitive tool: **Being in the waiting room**

You can help others by not getting so overly involved. That was the message I received from a Guide the other day. You can help in the kitchen without having to be one of the cooks. You help from afar while your loved one does all the work. It's also like sitting in the waiting room, being support, while the surgeons and the doctors do all the healing hands-on work treating your friend or loved one.

Don't carry it. Don't take it on. Don't feel responsible for it. Be supportive and loving, use that good duck energy, and take your place in the waiting room.

Remind yourself, they have guidance and helpers too. They are not abandoned, and you are not abandoning them by taking on a less direct position.

Hand it over and say, "You are capable. I believe in you. You take care of it," and let their team and God step in.

Problem 38: **Leaving your body**

Sensitive tool: **Grounding**

Lisa Campion has a great article on her blog about grounding and shielding for Empaths. She says that empaths, when overloaded, leave their bodies. I can attest to that!

During a period of time, whenever I felt emotionally attacked I'd find myself seeing a symbol and leaving my body to some astral place. From some detective work, I realized that this was a skill I learned in childhood when I had bad stomach problems and I didn't want to be in my body in pain. So, I'd find myself sitting next to the ceiling looking down.

This skill helps me in my work locate a lost animal or talk to someone who has passed, but doesn't need to be there in my everyday life. The tool needed here is grounding. I am stronger when I stand tall and firm in my space. Once I felt less vulnerable and stronger and was able to speak my feelings, I left less and less.

Feeling your legs and reaffirming that you are safe is the tool to use here. Carry a tourmaline rock in your pocket. Its healing qualities will pull you right back in and keep you on the earth.

It's also important to notice, where and with whom you feel this urge to leave. Why are you feeling unsafe? Can you speak your mind or your fears to that person? Perhaps, empathically you are registering that this person is unsafe for you. Honor this as best you can, limit your exposure, and then always make sure there is extra protections for you put in place whenever you have to deal with this person.

Problem 39: **Seeing only the surface**

Sensitive tool: **See below the surface**

When you work on your problems or issues you are having with other people, use your empathic ability to feel into what is the truth. Reality is rarely just what you see on the surface.

Let's say there's an office meeting where it is discussed that workers are stealing pens.

In one instance, a worker used a pen to jot down a note, forgot he had it, and simply threw it into his briefcase absentmindedly. He had no intention of stealing it.

Another man has been stealing pens every day since he's been in the job. He's using them to create a giant fort of pens at home.

One woman actually has a problem as a kleptomaniac and steals many, little things she sees. This is because her family was so poor growing up that she always fears she won't have what she needs. When she takes, she is in a little girl head space that never healed.

Another woman knocked over a pen from her desk when her coffee spilled, and it fell into her open bag on the floor. She didn't even know she had a pen from the office.

We live in a world that wants to only see the surface. I hate to say it, but many people are pretty shallow. This small perception makes some lives easier to handle. We read about celebrity romances falling apart and we assume we know why from the tiny facts we are given. But there is always a depth of layers of a bigger story underneath. Like the workers in the office, each person has a different motivation and reason behind their behaviors, and therefore, a different story. It's those different stories that make life interesting.

Use your empathic and intuitive abilities to always go deeper. Don't jump to the first conclusions by what you see. Things are rarely how they appear. Expand your world and be a detective.

~

Problem 40: **Folks that don't listen**

Sensitive tool: **Yellow energy**

I'm sure you've had the experience of the "bad hairdresser." You explain that you want a little off the sides, no bangs, and only an inch off the length. You get distracted reading a magazine only to look up and see the horror of bangs, five inches off the length, and a really bad haircut. She wasn't listening.

We all have folks in our lives that never listen. They are too busy hearing themselves talk, or the voices in their heads are so loud and continuous, it's hard to hear you. It's a real gift to be present for someone and hear what they are communicating, especially when they are speaking their truth.

The important part of this equation is when you speak your truth, whether you are saying how you feel or that something hurts, that you are being heard. If someone is hurting you and you tell them to stop, that person is SAFE, if they stop and listen. If they can't hear you, and dismiss you or throw it onto you, right now they aren't SAFE.

In my one online *Care of the Sensitive* fairy class I teach, I write about Yellow Energy. Embodying Yellow Energy is embodying your truth. Your energy does not have to go into trying to convince someone of anything, or force them to agree with you. They just need to honor your truth. And if they don't, walk away, for now, or create some strong boundaries. They may get it later. They may never get it, and it is not worth the energy in trying to help them understand. But, you are honoring yourself.

Problem 41: **Spiritual perfectionism & being hard on yourself**

Tool: **Be human**

As Sensitives, we can be very hard on ourselves.

I must say, it is spiritual to be cranky. And to be mad, or upset, or sad. It's all included in the package of being human. Lucky us. *The Secret*, is a great book, but the problem that came with it is many of us think we have to only think positively all the time or we attract bad stuff. That's a huge burden to carry, and most of the time that only means repression of the yucky thoughts.

You will have times in life where things just suck. It's the up and down of life we can count on. Right now, my life is in topsy-turvy and the last month, in some ways, has sucked. Most of my best buds are going through the same thing. I do like to focus on the positive end of it; the lessons being learned. But, I also have felt FRUSTRATED, ANGRY, UPSET, SAD, REALLY PISSED, and a bunch of other not very pretty things. But, you know what? That's good! That is a natural reaction to loss, and experiencing big changes. In order to get to the other side of the tough stuff, sometimes you need to barrel right through and feel it. THEN you get to the lessons and the gifts.

My mom used to remind me that I need to talk out my feelings and thoughts, and then I come to my own answers. That usually involves expressing all the poo underneath. Neither of my friends or my husband say to me, "Oh how very un-spiritual of you, Ronni. You should only express good things." Yes, I need to say what I want. But sometimes, you need to let out and express what you don't want to find out what you do.

Problem 42: **I'm sensitive to things**

Sensitive tool: **Being more careful what you take in**

As a sensitive, I am sensitive to many things. It's not that I'm a little delicate flower who can't survive in the world, in fact, I'm quite strong. My body is fine-tuned and knows when something toxic shouldn't be in there. For instance:

- My body seems to know when added MSG is in my food. My head will hurt, I will feel spacey, and a little woozy. I once had an MSG high for an hour in a Chinese restaurant. On hindsight, I think that this is probably a good thing. Why would I want a chemical unknowingly added to my food?

- Extra perfumes in my makeup or lotions beware! I will rash in protest.

- Lots of bad stuff in the milk or meat? I'll be the first to let you know.

- Someone just cleaned the store I just walked into with toxic chemicals? On comes the sneezing.

I look to my dog, Sarah, who has been losing some senses, and therefore, becoming more sensitive to the outside world. Recently, I used a carpet cleaner that gave her an allergic reaction. Her head puffed up! What if, I thought, she is showing me these chemicals aren't good for me either?

I used to think that there was something wrong with me. But what if there is something wrong with our world and how it is changing? Are we supposed to be all chemically enhanced and just be okay with it? Have we gotten so numb to our environment we don't even react to what is toxic in it? And this applies to all aspects of our lives. Becoming more aware and awake is a good thing. Becoming more sensitive, then, is also.

Problem 43: **Being rushed!**

Sensitive Tool: **Own rhythms and baby steps**

Being both creative and a sensitive means I am highly imaginative, maybe even with a hint of dramatic, which means I overwhelm easily. I already take in so much information on a deep level every day. Too much chaos around me equals chaos inside of me. And of course, I easily take on a great deal that isn't mine.

As a creative, I always have 3000 ideas for projects running around in my head. That is a very cool thing if I was three people in one.

There needs to be a healthy balance.

The big guidance I am getting is to create baby steps so I don't overwhelm and freak myself out. Here's an example.

It's time to make big changes in my life health-wise. I am completely addicted to sugar to keep up my hummingbird-like energy. So, I see the mountain ahead of me. Since I like climbing mountains I start to plan. I will get rid of all sugar in the house. I will substitute with healthy alternatives. I won't buy dessert at dinner at the restaurant. Yeah. Right. This will last for about five minutes before the panic sets in and I will finish that box of leftover Christmas cookies. I've just raised the bar so much that I won't succeed.

It's Monday and the new year, so it's time now to do all my business goals right now. I will start my whole way of doing things in a new way all today. In fact, this week I will manifest my new publisher and create the full proposal and finish my healing deck. I will be completely organized with my scheduling. I will create ten new doors to opportunity.

PANIC. Where are the cookies?

Baby steps make more sense. Even if you realized you need a new job, new career, new anything, you will still get there one step after another. There is no reason to overwhelm, or put that much pressure on yourself unless you are one of those overachieving, motivating speakers who seem to have superpowers or a good supply of amphetamines. (I doubt highly these folks are empaths.) For sensitive and creative people who tend towards this behavior, remember that change needs to happen slowly and steadily. What we really fear is the drastic and that's not what we want to create. We've had enough of that kind of change in the past years, why hurt ourselves?

You need to find your own unique rhythm at a pace that works for you.

As a child, I was always going against my own rhythms and following others' that didn't fit me. I always rushed.

I remember as a kid, my family and I would visit the local skating rink. Bold in athletics, I am *not*. It takes forever for me to dive in. I had my own approach skating. First, you stand in your skates. Then you hold on to the wall for a while. You progress to skating along the wall. Eventually, you branch out to skating in the middle of the rink and actually start to have fun. That's usually the time you have to leave and go home! This I learned, is my rhythm with pretty much every endeavor I attempt.

I may be more of the tortoise than the hare, but I get where I need to go. I love Nature because Winter isn't rushed, so there's Spring. There's time for everything. There are steps.

What's your next baby step?

~

Problem 44: **Other people projecting their fears onto you--
another form of carrying.**

Sensitive tool: **It's not about you**

Sarah had a bad case of Canine Peripheral Vestibular Syndrome,
where an elderly dog will lose their balance, the head tilts to one side,
and the eyes go back and forth. It's scary to watch, but does subside in
most cases. In Sarah's case, she was still battling vertigo and the head
tilt weeks later.

I posted the issue on my Facebook wall, and attracted more fear I was
already feeling.

One old friend warned me that her sister's dog died from this, and her
own dog was maimed for life, and I should take Sarah's condition very
seriously.

My panic rose to new heights.

A talk with a very rushed veterinarian scared me even more when she
said it could be a tumor or a problem that will probably get
progressively worse and I shouldn't feel guilty if I need to make the
decision to put her down. (Yes, this vet showed awful bedside manner
and tact. Needless to say, I now go to a different vet.)

When I tuned into guidance, I kept hearing that her condition wasn't
that serious and was treatable, but I couldn't honor that because I was
lost in the overwhelming fear. That old Facebook friend threw her fear
at me and it landed right on top of me, as did the vet's. As an empath, I
took it on. Fear attracts fear.

What's that quote? Fear equals false evidence appearing real.

This experience has been part of a long line of experiences helping me
learn not to take things personally and trust my own guidance. People,
even well-meaning people, will project their fears onto you. They talk
from what they know and has happened to them, and are trying to be

helpful. Others, hear your experiences and give advice that reflects their own beliefs and thoughts that don't reflect your own. They may not be able to look past their own experiences, especially if they haven't fully dealt with them. We all have our own filters we see through.

Telepathically and empathically, you can be so sensitive that throughout the day you can have foreign thoughts and fears flood you. It's a little like the "knowing who is going to call before they call" syndrome.

How do you protect yourself? It's a constant reminder: "It's not about you." Becoming very clear of what you feel and think will help you differentiate what isn't yours when it comes at you. Using your empathic ability, tune in to see what is going on with that person. Perhaps they have a great deal of fear surrounding doctors from a bad hospital experience at an early age, when they warn you to stay away from hospitals. That friend who tells you not to date a new friend who is a doctor can't see past her horrible divorce from a surgeon and is replaying those feelings in her head when she is giving you advice.

And incidentally, I was led to use homeopathy for Sarah and her vertigo from a friend who is a naturopathic doctor who suggested it. Within one month her vertigo went away and her head stays relatively upright most of the time. I've concluded from animal communication that she suffers from allergies that can aggravate the inner ear. And yes, my guidance was correct. It wasn't that serious.

Remember, it's about *them*.

~

Problem 45: **Life lessons repeating**

Sensitive tool: **Broken Leg theory**

I have a really cool set of spiritual Guides and Helpers. They put up with a lot when they signed up for being my Guides. In the past year, I have been irritable and nasty and have screamed at them many times, but their guidance has continued to help me through most of the challenges.

I wanted to know why I had to live through such a traumatic year, as have many of my friends and loved ones. I know all about the theories of life lessons speeding up as we get closer to 2012, so we have a great deal of "stuff" to tackle and get rid of. My Guides, always simple and to the point, but profound, explained to me the Broken Leg Theory. If you broke your leg ten years back, and it never really set in place correctly, when it rains you hurt tremendously. You still can't walk in a straight line without wobbling a little to the left. That's because it never healed. You may have barreled through the healing process and didn't attend to your needs or your feelings.

Right now, in our lives, we are being asked to heal all the proverbial broken legs that never set right--the issues we ignored and stuffed down, the childhood stuff that affected us throughout adulthood, and the patterns we never addressed. It isn't pretty. It's all up. It's our last chance to really heal.

Problem 46: **Carrying is not caring**

Sensitive tool: **Affirmation for Empaths**

"Even though you can feel it,
doesn't mean you have to fix it."

Another variation: "**You didn't create the problem that someone
created, so you can't be the one to fix it.**"

"**That's their lessons.**"

"**Carrying is not caring.**"

Problem 47: **Virus alert**

Sensitive tool: **Recognizing a virus**

Virus alert! Virus alert!

How do you know when your system was invaded by negativity coming at you? Our computers tell us that a virus has intruded. We need to look at our emotional and physical signs for evidence.

Does your energy feel lower? Do you feel like you are crashing? Are you suddenly depressed, fearful and insecure? Feel like there is a dark cloud over your head? There is. You've been bombarded with energy. This can happen when you are exhausted and your guard is down. Empathically, you've sponged the feelings and took it in.

You can get bombarded by the computer and the onslaught of negative input or sights. You may have someone in your energy like I did with the psychic vampire. Or, you are connecting telepathically with a love one through the cord you share between you and are taking on his/her feelings.

The tool here is to recognize it. Call it when it happens. Then tune in and see if what you are feeling is actually yours or not. Ask that whatever isn't yours to leave. Use the clearing methods mentioned in this e-book. None of this works? Unfortunately, it just might be your own funky mood.

See also tool #23, Depression

Problem 48: **Energy leaks and poor boundaries**

Sensitive tool: **Year-end Manifesto**

I just had a birthday. I was guided to make a personal birthday manifesto. (No, not like the Unabomber.) This long list would be culled from clues from my many journals that I keep track of my life in.

It is here where I decide what to get rid of in my life and what I shall keep in the coming year. And you may very well relate to my list. Consider writing one of your own to end out your year.

Include in your manifesto:

- List the areas where you continually are either a/triggered b/upset c/angry or d/just plain unhappy or bitch about, and translate those into boundaries of what you won't allow into your life. Create some powerful walls to protect yourself.

- List the areas that made you happy, smile, and feel good about yourself and life. These are the must-have's; the fuel for your tank. These are the things that no matter how busy life becomes you will include these or you will see a lack of balance and an unhappy you. It's a way to stay on path and on track.

- List regrets. Life is just a series of learning. Our regrets over the last years are what we would have done differently if we had a time machine. Listing these in no way is a vehicle to "should" on yourself. It's rather a great way to show how you have grown or learned in the past year.

- Goals. These are tricky. Many times, in the beginning of the year, we make a ton of wants and goals and then feel like crap by the end of the year when we didn't lose those 10

> pounds or publish our novel. I'd suggest this part be what
> you'd love to do or experience. Make it doable and possible.

Here are examples from my Manifesto. I have to have to be happy and what I won't give up:

1. my own pace and rhythms

2. quality time with those I love

3. teaching my on-line classes. Totally dig my students.

What I will give up:

1. shame from other people

2. giving to those that don't appreciate it

3. ignoring my own needs

Writing a year-end manifesto can make some powerful changes in your life as you shape what you want your world to be like. It also can help you stay more in-tuned to what *you* want, which for most empaths, is hard to do. We are wired to be in-tuned to those around us and our environment first.

~

Problem 49: **Catching a bad mood**

Sensitive tool: **Walk away**

You can feel someone else's mood a mile away, and it affects you like it would the smell of bad perfume. I learned an important lesson yesterday I wanted to share about setting boundaries and bad moods.

I took a detour yesterday and went to a different post office then my cozy, friendly one. I had to send a package via Customs and waited patiently in line. I had a few more packages fumbling under my arm that had to go to the States.

When I made my way to the Teller I felt it: Bad mood.

She looked at my package and told me curtly that it needed a Customs form. She talked to me like I was a moron and I was purposely insulting her. She then threw the form at me with no directions and brushed me away. Thinking logically, I asked her if I could just pay for the other packages and then fill out the form and she said no twice. That wasn't how it was done.

The form came in a little booklet with lots of pages and made very little sense when you are in a hurry. I filled out the end form thinking that was the procedure and went back in line to face her again. This time I had the growing sensation of insecurity building up inside of me. *"Was I stupid?"* I stopped my train of thought quickly and sized up the situation. No, this woman had an "everyone is a moron but me" attitude going that I did not appreciate and it was affecting how I felt. I almost took it on.

Back in front of her, I lost my temper when she chastised me for only filling out the last form, without realizing that it was a duplicate and I should have filled out the first form.

"How the hell would I know that?" I snapped at her. I had been virally affected by her bad mood, and now I was hostile and on the defensive.

I walked away back to the desk to fill out the form "right." That's when the "aha moment" arrived. Eureka! I could walk away. I could take my stuff and go to another post office or even wait for another teller in line. I mumbled this out loud. I didn't have to put up with her bad treatment or the bad mood she was flinging at others! I also didn't have to get involved with defending myself or confronting her and showing her what she was doing. That wasn't my job.

That's when the Universe rewarded me immediately for my new lesson learned. The woman was so riled she walked into the back and was replaced by another teller who now was about to serve me.

This woman fawned over my cute little drawn mailing labels and stickers and complimented me. We chit-chatted about making art and how much we loved the process, and she told me about her art. When the transaction was completed, she said "Nice meeting you."

This was a 180 degree turn around from what I had just experienced! I told the world what I wanted and what I didn't want. And I threw what wasn't mine back at the person and basically said, "Here. This isn't mine, it's yours." I won't put up with bad treatment.

Now I do understand that working at the post office is a very stressful job. My husband worked there for years and told me the counter was the hardest job of all. And I am always trying to understand where the other person is coming from and have compassion. But the teller expected defiance, rudeness, ignorance, and received it, by being rude! Her foul treatment passed along to me, and if I had owned her mood, caught that contagion, I would surely have passed it to many others throughout the day like a bad cold.

See it, just say No, and Yes to what you do want.

~

Problem 50: **No alone time**

Sensitive tool: **The Most Important Tool!**

The best way to overload as an empath is to spend your entire day surrounded by other people and their demands, wants and needs. See if you can function at the end of the day. Feel the exhaustion, the heaviness, and the confusion. You might even feel panic or fear, which is a symptom of overload. It is no longer just you in your space or aura, but many, many people. It gets crowded in there.

The most important tool for an empath is to have some alone space or time at the end of the day. This is mandatory. You need some time where you just feel you and your thoughts. Everyone needs to be cleared out of you.

This may not be always possible if you have a big family or a demanding mate, but there are techniques to squeeze this in.

My mother always took a bath after work at the end of her day. We kids always wanted to interrupt, but a bath is something that creates a natural, clear boundary.

Walking in nature also gives you time alone and is something that others won't question.

I used to think sitting and watching television gave me that needed space, but not if I am empathically tuning into the characters and their stories. (see problem #10)

Naps and sleeping work well also for squeezing in alone refreshing time. My favorite tool is writing in my journal at the end of the day. I am able to center back to me and see my feelings on paper. How can you incorporate this important tool into your life?

~

I hope you enjoyed and are now using the 50 tools
for the sensitive.
I am honored to share them with you.

I encourage you to head on over to my website and sign
up for my popular newsletter, and to explore and enroll in
Fairy Online School, where you can develop your natural,
psychic, empathic abilities. *The Care of the Sensitive* class
is very popular and helpful for empaths.

Fairy blessings,

Ronni, Designing Fairy

~

About the Author

Ronni Ann Hall, a.k.a. Designing Fairy

I am a psychic/spiritual teacher and animal/spirit intuitive empath who loves to share what I've learned and experienced through my stories and art.

I've been an empath and a sensitive since I was born, and I do believe that we are wired that way, and environment reinforces those abilities. I came across these tools in this book by experience and lessons learned, and by writing these down, it's my hope that you will benefit from the tools without having to experience the trials.

As a teacher, I like to help other empaths to embrace and expand their abilities. Because I am also a professionally-trained artist/designer, and a natural storyteller, I love to teach through my fun, illustrated, international Fairy Online School classes in Psychic Communication and Fairy Healing. I also offer teleclasses, private lessons and mentorships, a podcast radio show, flower essences, and a Healing Fairy Alphabet deck.

I've been a practicing teacher and intuitive professionally since 1999, when I opened my animal communication practice, *Dogbunny Animal Talk*. I've taught animal communication on-line and at the local college, Yavapai Community College, for many years. I later expanded my learning and teaching to healing with the fairy world, communicating with spirit and Angels, and offering tools to the Sensitive.

I'm also a proud, animal mom.

Offered at my website:

Fairy Online School: http://thedesigningfairy.com

Certification programs in Spirit Reader, Fairy Healer and Animal Communicator.

In progress: **The Healing Fairy Alphabet deck**, as well as,

Book 2 in the series: **The Turtle Shell**.

Made in the USA
Lexington, KY
20 December 2014